Connecticut
AN EXPLORER'S GUIDE

KIMBERLY GRANT

The Goodspeed Opera House in East Haddam, a Victorian jewel overlooking the Connecticut River, showcases American musicals.